I WAS There THE FIRST Christmas

written by Sandra Brooks

illustrated by Helen Endres

Library of Congress Catalog Card No.90-72095
Copyright © 1991 by Sandra Brooks
Published by The STANDARD PUBLISHING Company, Cincinnati, Ohio
Division of STANDEX INTERNATIONAL Corporation. Printed in U.S.A.

I'll never forget the first time I saw Mary. She was the most beautiful girl I'd ever seen. It wasn't just because her face was beautiful. She was beautiful from the inside out.

I never heard Mary say or do
anything mean or cruel to anyone, man
or beast. I never saw her lose her temper
or refuse to do her share of the work.

Now you know what I mean when I
say she was beautiful from the inside
out. But I wasn't the only one who knew
Mary was beautiful. God knew it too,
and He had a special plan for her as
soon as she was old enough.

Of all women in the world, God chose Mary to be His Son's mother.

At just the right time, God sent an angel to tell Mary about His plan. A few weeks later Mary was married, and her whole life changed.

Mary's neighbors had always thought she was a nice girl. Now they whispered cruel things behind her back.

They said, "It's much too soon for Mary to be expecting a baby. She hasn't been married long enough. She isn't the good person we thought she was."

Their words hurt Mary, but she forgave them. She knew she hadn't done anything wrong. Her neighbors just didn't understand God's plan. They didn't know her child was no ordinary baby. They didn't know He was the Son of God!

The months before Jesus' birth were long and hard for Mary. Then something happened to make it seem even longer and harder.

A few days before Jesus was born, Mary had to take a long trip. This was because the governor had ordered all the people to go to their own hometowns to be counted and taxed.

That meant Mary had to ride a donkey a long distance along a rough and rocky road. And lately she tired so easily. But at least she could rest at home. Now she couldn't.

During the trip I wondered why someone as kind and gentle and generous as Mary had to suffer so much. But I knew I could trust God to make it turn out right even though I didn't understand.

When Mary arrived in Bethlehem, she needed to rest, but there was no place to go. People were everywhere! Every house, every room, every corner was filled with people who had come home to be counted and taxed. Who on earth could help Mary?

Only God. And that's just what He did. Someone told us about a stable. "You're welcome to use it. It's not much, but it's better than nothing."

Mary rejoiced! She had trusted God to take care of her, and that's just what He'd done. Now she had a place to rest. Now she had a place for God's Son to be born.

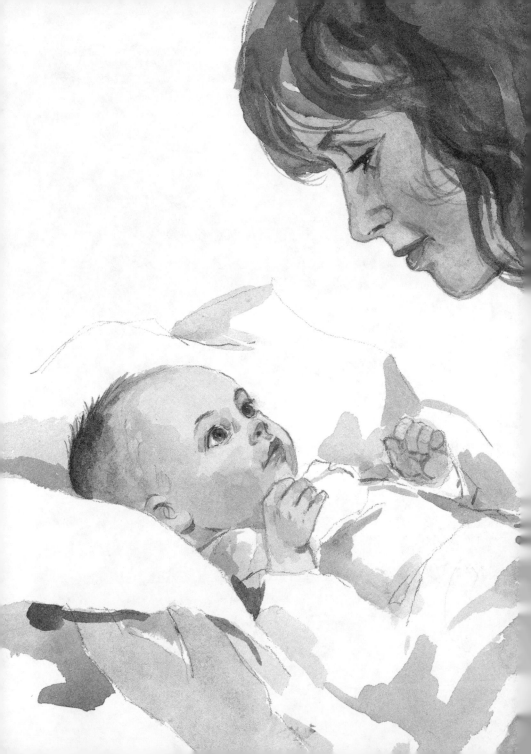

The night air was clear and cold when
the world first heard baby Jesus' voice.
Mary wrapped Him in swaddling
clothes and laid Him in a manger. Yes,
God had provided everything they
needed. Even a cradle for His Son.

Of course, none of us knew what lay ahead for this little baby. We couldn't have guessed He would grow up to be the Savior of the world. That His birth would change people's lives forever.

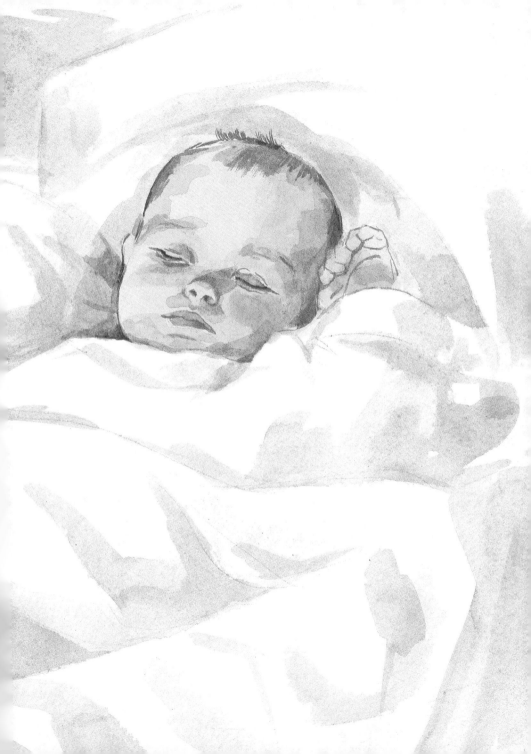

I guess you wonder who I am, and how I know so much about Jesus and Mary. I lived with Mary and Jesus. I was there when Jesus learned to walk and talk. I taught Him to build tables and chairs and other things made of wood. My name is . . .

. . . Joseph the carpenter.